Searching For California

Searching For California

The Story Of A 1960 Bicycle Road Trip

Bill Angus

2017

iv

In memory of Cecil and Lexi

Contents

The author, age seventeen, in the summer of 1958.

Changing Course

I was kneeling on the floor in Rettke's Garden Center in downtown Flint, carefully and meticulously cleaning aquarium tanks for eighty-five cents an hour. It was May 1960. I was nineteen years old and without a plan. I'd had a plan, one that came to me in a moment of clarity two years earlier. But nothing was clear now.

Let me explain. In April 1958 I was a senior in Flushing High School, due to graduate in six weeks. I was never an attentive student. In high school my full-time interest was hot rods. I worked tirelessly on my '51 Olds and I held a part-time job, evenings and weekends, pumping gas and working on cars in a Standard Oil service station. A son of the blue-collar world, I had no sense of career entitlement, nor had I any plan for my future.

Then, one particular April afternoon, life shifted. I was sitting in Mr. Fox's English class looking

out the window into an empty schoolyard, trying to imagine the world without classrooms. At
that moment it came to me, as suddenly as the
truth came to Saul on the road to Damascus, that
some of my classmates, those familiar strangers
seated around me, were making plans for the future. Some, like the girl with the bright red hair
standing at the front of the class giving a book
report, were already admitted to college for the
fall semester. They would be leaving high school
on a path into that world beyond the window that
I could never follow. My path, with a 1.7 GPA and
no plan, would leave me on a factory floor. In the
space of fifteen seconds, I converted. I changed
course. I decided I too would go to college.

I did not wait for graduation day. I found my
way to Flint Junior College and secured a pro-
bationary enrollment and a full load for the fall
semester. My FJC student advisor—Mr. Bob Smith,
an honest man—informed me that although the
admission test indicated I could do well in college, he had reviewed my high school record and
concluded that I would not succeed.

Skeptics were everywhere. On the last day of
classes at Flushing High School, I stopped by the
classroom of my English teacher, Mr. Fox, to tell
him the news that I had enrolled in FJC. I liked
Mr. Fox. He seemed to enjoy and encourage every student, even the poor ones. I told him the
good news as he sat at his desk in the empty

classroom. He looked at me for a few seconds, trying to absorb what he had just heard, before he responded, smiling as he always did, "Well, it will be a good experience for you anyway."

To be fair to Mr. Fox, the judgment he hung on me in that last word, "anyway," was not his alone; it was universal. My teachers, parents, and friends all had the same opinion: that I just wanted to stay in school rather than face the world. In fact, the opposite was true. I had suddenly decided, for the first time, to attend school. My purpose now was to find the world and search for my place in it.

My April epiphany was the real thing. In college I worked like a demon. In my first semester I earned a 3.5 GPA. In my second semester I was invited to participate in the honors program. In nine months I transformed myself from an aimless hot-rodder to an academic scholar. Mother and father were as proud as they were surprised. "He's going to college, and earning A's. This is crazy!"

I returned to college for my sophomore year an academic success. I had proven to my own satisfaction that I could go to college and do well. I had redefined myself—no small feat.

But now a problem emerged: I had no idea what I wanted to do. No career beckoned from the pages of the college catalog. My motivation to work tirelessly on every course began to wane.

Some required courses didn't interest me. Why was I even in college? I began to fear that I would not keep up the hard work and good grades and ultimately might fumble my one accomplishment: academic success. Confused and worried, at the end of my third semester I dropped out of college.

⟲

   Mother and Dad were confused too. I tried to explain that I had not given up on learning. On the contrary, I had prepared a list of twenty-two books on subjects that interested me—my own curriculum, as it were—which I would proceed to read during the winter and spring. Some of these books I had noticed students reading in other classes. Some I came across myself. I repaired to my room and began to read.

   My program of reading was going well, if slower than expected, when a problem emerged. One evening a friend of my father's came by. I was in my room reading while they were talking in the kitchen, when I heard my dad say, "He had better start being productive."

   I took a job at Rettke's Garden Center in Flint. My parents were relieved. So there I was, cleaning aquariums, when I heard Mr. Rettke's voice complaining loudly that I was taking too long to clean his fish tanks at eighty-five cents an hour. He hadn't complained when he sent me to his home to clean out his dog kennel, but that was before he raised my pay by a nickel per hour. I had dropped out of college, my reading program was going slow, and now my father's notion of "being productive" had lost its appeal. I finished cleaning Mr. Rettke's fish tank, walked down to his office, and quit. It was time for a change. It was time to break free, and I had an idea, something entirely my own: I would bicycle to California.

The decision to ride a bicycle to California didn't emerge fully developed in the moment. It had been gestating for six years. The idea first came to me in the fall of 1954 as I began the ninth grade. I came down with pneumonia and was home sick for three weeks. Although a poor student, I always enjoyed reading. In those three weeks, without school in the way, I read anything I could get my hands on.

A friend of my mother's brought over an armload of back issues of *Reader's Digest*. In one of those issues I read the story of a businessman who each year sponsored a young boy on a month-long bicycling trip in Europe. The businessman paid the youth's passage to Europe and gave him a stipend of seventy-five dollars for expenses. The adventure of bicycling through Europe, exploring the castles, villages, and historic cities, would enrich the young man's life and broaden his understanding of the world.

The idea burned itself indelibly into my

ninth-grade mind. I did not foresee a business-man showing up with passage to Europe, so I adapted the idea to my circumstances. If Europe was not available to me, California was; people had been trekking to California since the Gold Rush. I could bicycle from Michigan to California. Occasionally I would suggest my idea to a friend: "Hey, when we get out of high school, let's bicycle to California." There were no takers.

Now, in May 1960—six years after the inspiration of that *Reader's Digest* article—the time had come. I would bicycle to California, not only to fulfill that boyhood dream, but also with an unspoken hope that in the progress of such a journey I might find direction for my life.

I spent about a month preparing for the trip. My bicycle was a three-speed purchased at a Montgomery Ward department store a few years earlier. After WWII lightweight bicycles with three speed gear hubs began to be imported from England. They were commonly referred to as English bikes. My English three-speed had a black frame with white trim and chrome fenders.

In preparation for the trip, I built a cargo carrier to fit over the rear wheel. It was fabricated out of lightweight electrical conduit and covered with surplus red car seat vinyl I had once purchased from Buick Salvage for a car customizing project. I made the carrier large enough to hold my clothes, food, cooking gear, a camera, and other travel necessities. As for lodging on the trip, that was easy—I would camp out. I sewed together my own small, one-man pup tent using light-weight canvas, which I attempted to waterproof. Finally, I purchased a military surplus sleeping bag, which I would lash to the front handlebars. Since dropping out of college in January, I had managed to read only eight of the twenty-two books in my personal curriculum. I packed half a dozen more of those books to read on the ride.

Looking back, I'd say I did well enough choosing the bike and fabricating the gear; but planning the trip, researching the route, selecting the point A's and the point B's, not so much. I was in Michigan and I was going to California. That was my plan, pretty much in its full detail. I had no specific destination; California was a place to be, a state of mind, not an address. I wasn't even sure how long it would take to get there. I only knew I had to be back in Michigan by the end of August, since I had decided to re-enter Flint Junior College in the fall. As for preparing myself physically, I did do some practice rides. My longest practice ride was twelve miles.

In life, vision matters more than planning, for the lucky. By mid-June 1960, I had been packed and ready to begin the journey for over a week, but I had not yet planned a start. I had not decided on a start day and time, and I had not picked a target destination for the first day. I was waffling over the route out of Michigan. Should I take the most direct route and head southwest from Flushing around the bottom of Lake Michigan, a route taking me through heavily populated areas with all the associated traffic? Or should I follow a longer, more indirect route that would take me north through rural Michigan, across the Straits of Mackinac into Michigan's Upper Peninsula before turning west?

It happened that on Friday, June 17, I heard that Al Roeske was home on leave. I drove over to see him. Al and I became friends in high school through our shared interest in hot rods. In our senior year, together with four other friends, we formed Flushing's first hot rod club, the Road Saints—no irony intended. Now he was a nuclear engineering technician in the Navy.

When I arrived at his parents' home, Al, his girlfriend Eleanor, and his parents were busy packing their cars to head up north to the family cabin at Huron Beach. Eleanor, now a student at the University of Michigan, had been the valedictorian of our high school graduating class. She was one of the students I was thinking of that April afternoon in our English class when I had my epiphany.

Soon I found myself standing in the Roeske kitchen, explaining the conundrum I faced—whether to go south through Illinois or north through upper Michigan. Al solved my problem in an instant. He said, "We're leaving in an hour. You can ride up north with us and start your trip from Huron Beach."

I immediately called my mother to tell her I'd be home in ten minutes to get my bike and gear and that I would be leaving for California in an hour. Mother was surprised. She wondered if I was doing the right thing, if I was really ready. She began to cry on the phone. I had accompanied my mother to the Episcopal Church in Flushing every Sunday from early childhood until I was seventeen. I had been part of all her Sundays, at first faithfully and then dutifully, until I declared, at age seventeen, that I was done with religion. Here I was again, leaving her for some unfathomable reason. I rushed home to pack my gear. Mother was concerned but accepted that I was indeed about to leave for California. Al picked me up and within the hour I was on the road north.

That evening we arrived at Huron Beach. The Roeskes were generous people. They gave me a ride of over two hundred miles to their cabin to get me started on my adventure, and then they offered me dinner and invited me to stay the night. It was a generosity I did not foresee when imagining this journey, but would discover again and again.

When his leave ended in about two weeks, Al

Standing on my left is Al Roeske. We are at the Roeske family cottage in Huron Beach, Michigan.

My bike leaning against the fender of Al's yellow Dodge.

would be reporting to a new assignment, a naval base in the state of Washington. He planned to drive his car cross-country to his new post. We discussed the possibility of meeting up on the road west so I could ride partway with him. I liked the idea, but we could not identify a place to meet, because he was not sure what route he would take and I didn't know where I would be in ten to twelve days. Still, the possibility, however slim, did provide me with some hope to cling to in the exhausting first week of my ride.

Al did another favor for me, almost as good as a ride to the coast: it was his idea to make a sign to hang on the back of my bike that read, "California or Bust, Flushing, Mich." That sign caught the attention of many curious people along the way and frequently brought offers of dinner and lodging or rides.

At last, on Saturday, June 18, after a late breakfast, some talking, and some picture taking, at about 1:15 in the afternoon, we said our goodbyes. Six years after I read the *Reader's Digest* article, I got on my bike and started to pedal. I was on my way to California.

About to depart Huron Beach, Michigan for California on Saturday, June18, 1960.

On the Road

I pulled out onto US 23, a two-lane blacktop road cutting a path through miles of pine forest as it followed Lake Huron's coastline toward the Straits of Mackinac. My first day on the road would take me to Michigan's upper peninsula, specifically the town of St. Ignace at the north end of the Mackinac Bridge. This would be a ride of fifty miles, or four times further than my longest practice ride.

The *Readers Digest* article hadn't mentioned headwinds. Nevertheless, I found myself pedaling directly into a stiff wind. Less than two hours into my cross-country journey, I began to feel exhausted and weak.

I came upon a roadside picnic table situated near a small gas station with a log cabin facade. I stopped to rest, stretching out on the picnic table bench. Lying down did not help. I began to wonder if I could even make it to the bridge on my first day. I walked over to the gas station, purchased a candy bar, and returned to the picnic table. To my surprise, as soon as I ate the candy bar, I began to feel stronger. Powered by two more candy bars, I pedaled on and reached the bridge. Food mattered, food and shelter, and they would matter every day.

At the Mackinac Bridge, a small example of what would become an endless list of my planning omissions revealed itself. I discovered that bicycling across the bridge was prohibited. No problem. I hitched a ride across with the driver of an old green pickup truck.

I had made it. I was in St. Ignace. Another mile or so and I would arrive at my destination, the home of my father's sister Lily and her husband, Frank Sharley. They operated a two-room tourist motel east of town on US 2.

Aunt Lily and Uncle Frank in St. Ignace.

The road is full of travelers. Aunt Lily, as a young girl, emigrated with her family—her parents and her six siblings—from Lancaster, England, to Flushing, Michigan. Frank, also English, was born in London. Lily and Frank met in Detroit and lived there until they retired, when they moved to St. Ignace and opened their motel. They welcomed me that evening. They fed me. They let me roll my sleeping bag out on their living room floor. The next morning, as I left, they took pictures and wished me well on my journey.

I left St. Ignace early Sunday morning, June 19, pedaling west on US 2 following the north shore of Lake Michigan. It would be another day of strong headwinds. On a three-speed bike low gear works for going up steep hills, slowly. High gear, or third gear, works for reaching higher speeds, if you are not going up a hill or into a headwind. Otherwise, it's second gear. By 9:45 a.m., I had already covered forty-five miles, mostly in second gear. I stopped to rest and have lunch. I would pedal another thirty miles before stopping for the day. For the first two days I was rarely able to use high gear.

It was only day two of this bicycle journey, but my sense of road etiquette had already changed. I would no longer consider giving up my right to the road's hard, smooth cement or asphalt surface. A few hours of pedaling into the stiff headwinds and up hills was enough; I would not compound the difficulty of this project by moving from the road surface onto the soft gravel shoulder merely to accommodate passing cars. Horns were honked. So what?

My first message home since my sudden departure the previous Friday was a postcard I mailed from the village of Naubinway on US 2. I made note that I was mailing this postcard on Father's Day and that I had gotten off to a good start, but that the weather was cold and windy. All my correspondence throughout the trip would be via the United States Post Office, a ubiquitous and dependable agency that swiftly delivered the mail to anyone with an address. That left me out, since I did not have an address. Consequently my correspondence was one-way. I mailed letters home to my folks every two or three days and occasionally sent postcards to friends and other family members. In 1960, mailing a first-class letter cost four cents and a postcard three cents. Only once on my ride west was I able to arrange to receive mail at a general delivery address. I could have called home from a pay phone, but given my budget, long-distance calls were far too expensive for routine updates and mere hellos. In 1960, smart phones, the Internet, web pages, and social media, in all their manifestations, were as yet undreamed of, except perhaps for Dick Tracy's wristwatch.

Toward evening, a little east of Manistique,

where US 2 comes near the shoreline of Lake
Michigan, I found a likely campsite, a deserted,
lightly wooded area sloping down toward the
lake. I wheeled my bike off the road twenty or
thirty yards toward the lake, until I was out of
sight of the road. I made a meal of another peanut butter and jelly sandwich and then rolled out
my sleeping bag. It would be my first night under the stars. Actually, I don't remember the stars.
I remember the mosquitoes. They were fierce.
Luckily, my army surplus sleeping bag was a
mummy-style bag. When zipped all the way up, it
completely covered my head and most of my face,
leaving just a small opening to breathe through.
I spent the night breathing in and spitting out
mosquitoes.

I woke up early to a cold, overcast day, packed
my gear, and wheeled the bike back on to US 2. I
planned to follow US 2 southward along the edge
of Lake Michigan at least as far as Menominee before turning west. I was barely into my third day,
and already I was imagining meeting Al in his
bright yellow Dodge somewhere in South Dakota.

A few hours on, a pickup truck stopped. The
driver said he was on his way to Iron Mountain,
and if I was going in that direction, he would be
glad to give me a lift. Iron Mountain was fifty miles
out of my way to the northwest. But my dad's
brother, my Uncle Bert, had moved to the Upper
Peninsula a few years earlier, and Iron Mountain

sounded like the name of the town where he lived. The possibility of sleeping indoors, behind screens, changed my plans. I took the ride.

After asking around Iron Mountain, I learned that apparently no one had ever heard of my Uncle Bert. It seemed that I might have confused Iron Mountain with another western Upper Peninsula town, either Iron River or Ironwood. I gave up hope of indoor accommodations and pedaled out of town.

As darkness settled, I found a city campground in Norway, seven miles southeast of Iron Mountain. I was relieved to find this small campground and still more pleased when the caretaker said he would not charge me for the night. Only a few campsites were occupied. I chose a site and rolled out my sleeping bag.

Nearby, a young couple appeared to be finishing their dinner. They invited me to join them at their campfire. They cooked my soup for me, gave me some crackers, washed my dishes, and—perhaps more important than either food or company— gave me mosquito repellent. We talked for a while. I found out they were from Ohio, and the husband had just been drafted. They were on a last getaway before he had to report to the army.

This first night in a campground offered a clue to just how valuable the sign that Al had scribbled on a piece of cardboard and tied to the back of my bike would become. The sign "California or

Bust" caught the caretaker's eye and caused him to waive the fee. The sign's proclamation also piqued the curiosity of the Ohio couple, prompting them to invite me to their campfire.

I was on the road by 7:30 the next morning, Tuesday, June 21. Within a few minutes I had crossed into Wisconsin, pedaling south on Highway 8. It was empty country. About ten miles into the ride, Highway 8 took a right turn to the west. There were no buildings, no houses, just a turn in the empty road among empty fields. I turned the corner. Pedaling away, I felt an urge to look back. Twisting around on the seat of the bike, I looked back to that turn in the road. My first objective in this unplanned road trip was to get around Lake Michigan. Turning that corner on Highway 8 put Lake Michigan behind me. I felt a brief moment of accomplishment. I was on my way west.

Later on, around noon, I stopped in Laona, Wisconsin, to rest. I wrote the following in a letter I mailed home the next day:

> *June 21, 1960*
> *Dear Mom and Dad,*
> *It is a miserable day, but no headwind. I left Norway at 7:30 this morning and made about sixty miles by 12:15. I am now taking a rest. I hope to make it to Rhinelander today, another forty miles. I hope I can make it; it's always harder in the afternoon due to the headwind. I am on highway eight now. It is not so great; mostly forest reserves. The only places there are houses are where there are towns on the map. Not many tourists travel the road so there are no camping grounds, and very few parks.*
> *I am sending some books home. I don't have*

time to read them and I could use the space.

Al says he may go the northern route, if he goes alone. I am supposed to let him know where I am so if he comes this way he can give me a lift. If he does stop I may take a ride. It would be cheaper and I would get to spend more time in California.

Sorry this letter is so short, but I want to spend all the time I can on the road, so I can get back to a tourist route somewhere in Minnesota. I expect to be in Minnesota the day after tomorrow. I will write on the twenty-third and let you know where I will be on the twenty-ninth so you can send a letter to arrive on that date.

   Love,
   Bill

Finding Shelter

Dwight Eisenhower was still President of the United States on the afternoon of June 21, 1960, when the wind shifted to the southeast along US 8 in Wisconsin. The Everly Brothers had the number one tune on the charts. Alfred Hitchcock's film *Psycho* had just been released a week earlier, and Vice President Richard Nixon was wrapping up a string of primary victories to become the Republican Party's candidate in the November presidential election. But none of that was on my mind. With the wind now at my back, I made sixty-five miles after my midday break instead of the forty I expected. By the time I reached Tomahawk, Wisconsin, around 8:30 p.m., I had been on the road thirteen hours and pedaled 125 miles, making this my first hundred-mile day. I was exhausted. It looked like rain, and my map showed no campground within reach.

I had left home with seventy dollars in my

pocket, hoping that would be enough to cover food and camping fees all the way to California. By now, I could see a few problems with my plan. For example, since I had little room to store food in my carrier, I found myself purchasing food as needed. Milk I would drink when purchased or soon after, since I had no cooler. This presented a problem in the sparsely populated forest reserves of northern Michigan and Wisconsin, and was one reason I tended to end each day's ride in a town where I could buy what I needed for the next day. Another example, campgrounds are not always where you need them. If I happened to be in the rural countryside as my day of pedaling ended, no problem—I could simply find a secluded spot, pull off the road, and roll out my sleeping bag, as I did along US 2 in the Upper Peninsula. But when the day's ride ended in a town or a small city without a nearby campground, just stopping and rolling out the sleeping bag on someone's lawn didn't seem like an option, and on my budget, motel rooms were out of the question. So as I entered Tomahawk—remember, this was 1960 in the rural Midwest—I thought I would go to the local police station to ask if they had an empty jail cell I could use for the night.

I found the police station and asked for the favor of a jail cell. My situation was not that desperate. The police directed me to a city park, one not on my map, about a half mile out of town.

Relieved, I rode on through town to the park. To this exhausted traveler, afraid of finding no place to sleep on a dark and rainy night, this park looked like the best campground I had ever seen. Circumstances may have influenced my first impression, but the Tomahawk Campground did provide everything I needed.

I signed in at the entrance, and the park caretaker directed me toward the campsites. There were only a few other campers. I chose a site and set up camp. I was tired and hungry. I prepared a couple of peanut butter and jelly sandwiches and drank the better part of a quart of milk.

A man camped nearby struck up a conversation, curious about the kid on the bicycle trip. Soon three young high school boys, who had seen me ride through town, came to the park looking for me. They had read my sign, "California or Bust." They had many questions. We talked about the route I planned to follow, how far I could travel in a day, when I thought I would get to California, and so on. I explained that I was looking forward to getting beyond the forested country and into farm country so I might find a few days of farm work and eat some good farm meals. Well, they left and came back in about fifteen minutes with two hamburgers, two hot dogs, two sandwiches, and a banana.

In the meantime, the fellow camping near me had already been giving me travel advice. He added that he wished he had done something like I was doing when he was young. Now he insisted that I roll out my sleeping bag in the campground's small, green octagonal bandstand in order to be sheltered from the rain. Since I couldn't pitch my tent on the bandstand's wood floor, he gave me a heavy blanket to keep me warm. I crawled into my sleeping bag, sheltered from the rain, warm, full of food, and ready to sleep.

Then three more kids—two from town and one from the campground—appeared. They came up the bandstand steps and sat on the floor; they wanted to talk about the trip. I crawled out of my sleeping bag. We sat on the wooden floor, in the dark, and for ten or fifteen minutes talked about bicycling to California. They left, but a few minutes later one came back to ask if I would like a fish dinner his folks had just cooked. No, I had to refuse. After eating all the food the others had brought, as well as two of my own sandwiches and a quart of milk, on top of being exhausted, the thought of more food made me ill.

In the morning I took a shower and began to pack. The caretaker came by my campsite to talk. He asked me to send him a card when I got to California, and said he would put in the local paper that I had stopped for the night in Tomahawk. He gave me back my camping fee—fifty cents, which was already half of the regular camp rate— and then handed me another dollar. He said if he had given it a second thought, he would have invited me to stay at his home. The camper who had helped me move into the bandstand the previous evening offered me another dollar and, as a breakfast treat, a cup of coffee and a bun. I was surprised at the interest the folks in Tomahawk had shown in my trip and thankful for their generosity, especially for the food. Tomahawk was sure a friendly town. I left late in the morning, about 11:00.

I used the two dollars to buy a hat. How could I have not thought to bring a hat? Fortunately I did bring a jacket, and so far I had worn it all day each day. Pedaling hard caused me to sweat continuously, and the constant wind chilled me. My wristwatch also proved unexpectedly useful. It served as my speedometer and my GPS. It was how I knew approximately where I was in those long, empty miles of forest, farmland, and later prairie.

For the next nine hours I followed Highway 8 due west through sparsely populated northern Wisconsin, arriving in the small farming community of Barron at about 8:00 in the evening. There was no campground near Barron. There was a city park large enough that it might offer a secluded spot to roll out a sleeping bag, but the park was crowded with people attending a softball game.

I considered going on to the next town—Taylors Falls, Minnesota—but that was forty miles further. I found a spot on Main Street where I could sit down and spend some time updating a letter home.

By the time I was caught up on recounting the news of my trip, darkness was settling. I rode back to the city park and took a seat in the bleachers to watch the final innings of the game, hoping that when it ended, the park would empty and I might find a place to roll out my sleeping bag. When the game finally did end and people began to leave the park, it occurred to me that in such a small town, a stranger sitting alone by the bleachers with his bike might seem suspicious, so I left too.

It was about 11:00 when I returned to the park. I pedaled quietly along the drive. No one was around. Soon I came to the park pavilion, dimly illuminated by a single nearby streetlight. It was a rectangular cement block structure with large, screened openings on all four sides, extending from the roof to about four feet above the floor. On each end of the pavilion was a screen door.

I rode by slowly, still seeing no sign of anyone in the park. I stopped at the far end of the pavilion and tried the screen door. It was unlocked, so I stepped inside. In the center of the pavilion, about eight feet from the outer walls, was a windowless interior room with a closed door. I opened the door and stepped into the dark space.

Only a faint sliver of light could be seen under another door at the opposite end. I felt the room was too dark and too contained to be safe, so I stepped out and closed the door.

I continued through the screened area toward the other end of the pavilion. Against the wall on either side of the screen door at the other end of the pavilion were two park benches. They were long enough to sleep on and hidden from view below the screens. I went back outside for my bike, then rolled out my sleeping bag on one of the benches and laid my bike down on the floor, out of sight from anyone passing by.

A picture of the Barron park pavilion taken years later on a trip through Wisconsin. The window screens and the screen door are gone.

I was about to crawl into my sleeping bag when a pair of headlights appeared. A car had turned into the park and was slowly coming along the same drive I had ridden my bike down a few minutes earlier. I watched the lights. As the car came nearer, I recognized that it was a police car. The police car came to a stop beside the pavilion. I was concealed in the shadows, but my first impulse was to step forward, reveal myself, and explain my circumstances, trusting in the police to be helpful. I began to phrase my story in my mind: "I'm on a cross-country bicycle trip. Since there is no campground nearby, I chose this park as a place to sleep for the night. I'll be on my way in the morning."

Two policemen stepped out of the car, their flashlights sweeping the night. At that moment, to my own surprise, I held back. I crouched down and stayed concealed. The two officers walked to the far end of the pavilion. They opened the same screen door I had entered through minutes earlier. They stepped in and opened the door to the inner room. A shaft of light darted out under the door at my feet. They stepped out and closed the door. Beams of light flashed up one side of the screened-in walkway, then the other. I waited to be found. An officer started to walk down one side of the screened area, his light flashing toward the end of the pavilion where I crouched. Then he stopped, turned, and left the pavilion. The two officers got into their car and drove away.

My relief was boundless. At the same time, I was aware of another feeling. I had chosen not to seek the officers' approval or defer to their authority. Alone, in a strange city, I had chosen to rely on myself. I felt free.

I pulled out early the next morning, Thursday, June 23. It was a cold, overcast day. No sooner had I left Barron on a forty-mile stretch to the Minnesota border than the rain started. Before I had traveled three miles, I was forced to take shelter. Waiting out the rain, I finished a letter home, updating my parents, sparingly, on my stay in Barron. I would mail it in Taylors Falls.

I arrived in Taylors Falls about 9:30 a.m. and set about to find the post office. By the time I located it, the rain had picked up again. I found myself trapped in the tiny front service area of the post office with my bike, waiting for the rain to stop. Fortunately, the postmistress was friendly and didn't mind that I was hanging around.

I waited from about 9:30 in the morning until 2:00 in the afternoon, venturing out briefly a couple of times. I spent most of my time reading *Walden, or Life in the Woods*. Why Thoreau? This was the one book I did not mail back home—not because I was enthralled with Thoreau, but because it was the smallest book I had packed; it took up so little space. Now Thoreau had become my rainy day reading.

The rain did not stop, but eventually it lightened and I decided to push on. I bought a cheap plastic raincoat and prepared to leave. I had learned that morning that when pedaling in the rain, my feet would get soaked from the spray coming off the front tire. To keep my feet dry, I covered them with plastic bags tied above my ankles. I like to think that's the kind of thing Thoreau might have done. The postmistress gave me a handful of pieces of wrapped candy, "for energy." I thanked her, said goodbye, and left the shelter of the post office. As I walked my bike along the sidewalk toward the street, I heard the postmistress call after me to wait. She ran into a store and soon emerged with a full bag of candy for me, insisting that the few candies she had first given me were not enough.

I had a fifty-mile ride ahead of me to reach Minneapolis. It was 2:00 in the afternoon. I wanted to arrive before nightfall, so I had no choice but to ride on through the rain. I was caught in heavy cloudbursts six times. At one point I was riding in a light drizzle as I passed into the shelter of a railroad viaduct. A few seconds later, as I pedaled out from under the viaduct, I rode straight into a downpour. The conditions could change that quickly.

I reached Minneapolis by 6:30 in the evening.

I had heard of places called youth hostels, which provide inexpensive lodging for young travelers, and that there might be one in Minneapolis. In the phone book I found a number for a youth hostel office, but no one answered. I then phoned the police department to find out the hostel's location (you get your money back when you call the police from a pay phone). I was told it was on the south side of town in the university district, so I rode to that area and eventually found the office. To my disappointment, they did not offer lodging. It was an office that helped university students and others arrange for lodging in Europe. They told me there were only two youth hostels in the United States that provided lodging for travelers: one in New York and one in San Francisco.

By now it was almost 8:00. Earlier, when I had talked to the police, they told me to ride to the general vicinity and then call them back for specific directions. Although I had found the hostel office myself without further help, I thought I should call the police back anyway, since I had told them I would. I stopped at a Standard Oil station to use the pay phone, after which I planned to pedal five miles to the west side of town and stay at the Minneapolis YMCA.

While I was on the pay phone, a man in his late twenties or early thirties stepped into the gas station. He had apparently taken note of the "California or Bust" sign still tied to the back of my bike.

Once I got off the phone, he began asking me questions about my trip. When I mentioned that I'd had no luck finding a youth hostel, he invited me to his apartment for the night. He worked in the theater department at the University of Minnesota. He explained that his wife was away and he would welcome the company. Perhaps an older, wiser traveler would have been more cautious, or perhaps a twenty-first-century nineteen-year-old would read his offer as a more layered invitation. But I took it at face value, as a generous offer of accommodation to a needy traveler.

His apartment was small. A kitchen, dining table, and sofa made up the living area, and all around were shelves stuffed with books. I took a shower. He cooked a warm meal of beans, sandwiches, and coffee. We talked about books and listened to his hi-fi. He was into Karl Marx. I knew little of Marx, but in an attempt at counterpoint, I shared what I had gleaned recently from the essays in David Riesman's *Individualism Reconsidered*. Finally, I lay down on the sofa in his small apartment and slept, warm and dry.

The next morning, Friday the 24th, I was up early. We had breakfast. I thanked my host for his generosity, said goodbye, and set out on my way.

It was sunny in the city of Minneapolis when I crossed the Mississippi River at about 8:00 in the morning. This far north, the Mississippi is not the mile-wide mythic force of story and song we all know. But it is the Mississippi, so I stopped on the bridge I was crossing to take a picture, looking south in the morning sun. On the east bank the river flowed past the university district, and on the west bank were storage tanks and piles of coal.

Crossing the Mississippi River in Minneapolis.

This was the first picture I had taken since leaving St. Ignace five days earlier. Wisconsin and Minnesota looked no different to me than Michigan, so I had found no reason to take pictures until now. I was focused on the destination, not the journey. Nevertheless, west of the Mississippi River the country did change. The forests of Wisconsin and Michigan disappeared. Now it was all farm country. The land was flat. The horizon was distant. Almost the only trees to be seen were a few planted around farmhouses. Occasionally I saw a thin line of trees along a creek. The farmhouses, each with a cluster of barns and sheds were spaced far apart, but I could see farm after farm into the distant horizon.

For the last forty miles of my ride that Friday, the unrelenting wind blew head-on. And now I was beginning to have trouble with the bike. The gear-hub was slipping out of high gear. If I put much pressure on the pedal while in third gear, the gear would slip free, the pedal would spin halfway around, then catch with a bang. Not only that, but a fender brace broke; it caught in the spokes, buckling the fender. Later a spoke broke in the rear wheel and the rear fender separated from the frame. I was able to wire the fender back onto the frame. The slipping gear-hub was a bigger worry.

I reached Redwood Falls, Minnesota, by 8:00 in the evening. Once again, a day of hard riding had left me exhausted. I asked at a service station if they knew of any nearby campsites. They did not. I decided to pedal on a little further, hoping to find a city park or at least a secluded spot outside of town where I could pull off the road and roll out my sleeping bag.

I have to laugh at my luck. I had just pulled out of the gas station when I noticed that a car had turned around and seemed to be following me. I knew that I looked like a vagrant on a bike in my dirty clothes, with a cardboard sign tied to my carrier, but I was tired and did not want to be hassled.

Sure enough, the man driving the Studebaker Lark signaled me to stop, so I did. He asked me a series of questions: where I was from, where I was going, how far I had traveled that day. I answered his questions, curtly at first, until he shared that he had bicycled in Europe.

My questioner was a local lawyer and bicyclist. He was on his way back to his office for some night work. I asked if he knew of a campground in the area. He did not, but he had a better idea: he invited me to his home to spend the night. He took me home, introduced me to his wife, got a meal started for me, and then went back to work. I enjoyed another hot meal, a shower, and a great night's sleep in a real bed. Rested, I left Redwood Falls around 9:30 in the morning after a good breakfast and a little repair work on my bike. That repair including fashioning a new "California or Bust" sign to replace the original sign, which the previous day's rain had left in remarkably poor shape.

This trip was the unplanned life in microcosm: a disaster and a gift. In preparing for the trip, I did not contemplate the obvious imperatives, such as the appetite that results from pedaling eighty to a hundred miles a day or the need for suitable clothing and plenty of water when cycling from sunup to sundown in the summer heat. Neither did I anticipate the social context of a cross-country bicycle trip. I was on a marathon ride to reach California. I did not think about meeting people along the way, much less that people would be interested in my trip.

People were interested. Some were curious at the spectacle of a kid trying to ride to California on a bicycle. For others, it was slightly more complicated—perhaps the memory of a youthful dream that went untried and lost. For my sake, thankfully, many kind and generous people noticed me and stepped forward to invite me into their homes, offering me food and a place to sleep. These were joyful intervals in a grueling journey.

The Minister and The Mechanic

The summer of 1960 was the last breath of the '50s. In May, Elvis Presley was discharged from the US Army. Cassius Clay was still Cassius Clay, and Vietnam, LSD, and hippies were over the horizon. Maybe it was a simpler country then, more trusting of a stranger on a three-speed bike with no money and no plan more substantial than the declaration "California or Bust" scribbled on a cardboard sign.

Saturday, June 25, 1960, was my eighth day on the road. I was determined to reach South Dakota by the end of the day. Brookings, the nearest town in South Dakota, was about ninety-eight miles from Redwood Falls, Minnesota. On a normal day, that distance, and a few miles further, would be doable. On this day, it turned out not to be so easy. A headwind in excess of twenty miles an hour blowing out of the southwest made every mile a struggle. By midafternoon I had made only thirty-seven miles. Not only was the wind taking a toll, but the temperature rose to well over ninety degrees. The backs of my hands, my forearms, and my ears were becoming badly sunburned.

I stopped in Marshall, Minnesota, to rest. I decided to wait there until evening in order to ride at night in the hope that the wind would die down, which it did. I put reflector tape on the bike's fenders and departed Marshall for Brookings, a distance of sixty miles. There was little traffic on Route 19 in rural western Minnesota late that night. I made it safely to Brookings by midnight.

June 25 had been a hard day. It had taken me fifteen hours to ride from Redwood Falls to Brookings. The bicycle's third gear problem continued to worsen. Given the headwind I had faced, it didn't matter much that third gear was not working that day, but it was essential for the rest of the trip. I could not pedal many hundred-mile days using only second gear.

Once in Brookings, I needed to find a place to sleep. Again, as I had in Tomahawk, Wisconsin, I went to the police station to ask if I could spend the night in a jail cell. Looking back, it may seem puzzling that I would view police stations as safe harbors. Maybe in the rural Midwest in 1960 the police were seen as supportive agents of the community, or maybe it was more about my Uncle Albert. Mother's brother Albert was the police officer in a small town in Ontario. I clearly remember going to his police station when I was a child. Uncle Albert would let me go into the jail cell, a bright, small cell with white walls, and then close the door. I was in jail—what fun! The Brookings Jail cell would not be as much fun, but I was thankful for the shelter. In my next letter home I related the outcome of my night ride out of Wisconsin.

> *Brookings, S.D.*
> *June 26*
> *Dear Mom and Dad,*
> *I made it to Brookings by midnight. The traffic was light and the wind had died down. I am in jail now. I could not find accommodations, so I tried the jail; they let me sleep in a cell. It was about my soundest night's sleep yet. It is about 7:00 a.m. now. I cannot get out until 8:00 a.m.*
> *I can hear the wind outside and it sounds as strong as ever. I am not going to travel at night. There are too few places to stop for food or a drink out here during the day; at night I might not find any. They say the next thousand miles are going to be very trying. My high gear broke down completely yesterday. I can only get about five turns out of it, and it slips. I can't use it too much in this wind anyway, but pedaling in second makes my legs tired, and for some reason, my knees, especially my right one, sore.*
> *The jailer brought me about half a cake (left over from a party) and two cups of coffee. I ate*

it all, of course. I drink more milk than ever. I started by drinking one quart a day, but it quickly went to two, and about the last three days I have drunk three quarts per day. I spend more on milk than on other food. I got two cans of pork and beans for 29 cents (for both) but I have not had to eat them yet. At one place, Morton, Minnesota, I got a half-gallon of milk for 30 cents. I have bought a quart for 18, 19, and often for 20 cents. I buy a lot of bread and jam and make sandwiches. I have gotten meat and eggs from the different people I have stayed with. The hardest part of the trip is not being able to eat enough.
Love, Bill

I thanked the two policemen on duty that Sunday morning for their help and kindness and turned my bike back toward Route 14, looking for a place to stop and work on the bike. I found a gas station open, where I spent some time making adjustments to the cable tension on the bike's gear selector. I left Brookings about 9:45 a.m. and pedaled for Huron, seventy-five miles ahead on Route 14. I hoped to travel fifteen or twenty miles beyond Huron. It was another day of high temperatures and strong wind, but today the wind was not in my face; it was blowing out of the south, at a right angle to the direction I was pedaling. It did not hold me back. Indeed, the wind helped to cool me as I pedaled westward under the hot sun.

Those long stretches, riding down empty rural highways in the early days of the trip, pedaling into persistent headwinds, always hungry, thinking about the emptier, longer stretches of highway ahead in the west, gave rise to many second thoughts about the whole bicycle-to-California idea. The challenge of the trip seemed overwhelming. Each day I would think about turning around and heading home. But the hope that I might meet up with my friend Al on the road ahead helped to keep me going through those first days.

Back when I was in Wisconsin, on the fourth or fifth day of the trip, I had written to my folks that I hoped to be in Rapid City by June 29 and that they could send mail to me in care of general delivery at the post office there. I also sent a postcard to Al with the same information. But I was guessing. I could not be sure how long the exchange of mail would take or how long it would take me to reach Rapid City. Later, when I was making good time in Minnesota, I began to worry that I might arrive in Rapid City early and find myself having to camp somewhere for one or two days to wait for the mail. As the miles added up, the idea of taking a couple of days off to rest became appealing, mail or no mail. So I decided I would stop in the Black Hills, near Rapid City, for a day or even two days of rest. Nor would this time-out be only for the rest, as much as I needed it. The hope still lingered that I might meet up with Al and catch a ride with him to the coast, shortcutting this whole miserable life-discovering experience.

As Sunday afternoon wore on while I was pedaling on Route 14, the sky turned an ominous yellow and storm clouds gathered to the west. This was tornado country. I started to be concerned. Then, five miles east of Huron, South Dakota, the bicycle's gear-hub failed completely. Now low gear and second gear were gone. I could pedal in high gear, but only if I applied very light pressure to the pedal, and even then the gear slipped badly. I made it into town and stopped at a service station to figure out what to do. Tornado warnings were up. I had one bit of luck: I had learned in Brookings that Huron had a good bike shop, and I found it in the Huron phone book. It was a Sunday, but when I called the number someone answered. I made an appointment for Monday morning.

Next, I needed to find shelter. Even if there was a campground nearby, camping out in a tornado was not an appealing option. I assumed there would be a jail in town, but first I checked the phone book for an Episcopal church. I found a listing that gave an address for the pastor, Reverend Donald West. I went to the rectory. As I stood knocking on the front door, Reverend West came bounding around the corner of the house.

He looked to be about thirty and wore a crew cut.

I briefly explained my situation, referenced my Episcopalian roots, and asked if I could roll out my sleeping bag in a Sunday school room at the church. "Sure," he said, "Let's go down to the church and take care of your bike." We walked to the church, where we put my bike and bedroll in a classroom. Then he invited me back to his home for dinner.

Walking back, we exchanged introductions. He told me he had attended seminary in Philadelphia and that his wife was from that city. It surprised me that he recognized a Canadian accent in my voice. I explained that my mother was Canadian and that I had spent most of my childhood holidays and summers in Canada with her family.

Reverend West mentioned that the church congregation had picnicked that afternoon. He and his wife had brought home an abundance of leftovers, more food than I could imagine, he said. Well, anyone eating on a dollar a day while pedaling across country becomes good at imagining food. But he was right—there was an abundance: chicken, potatoes, rolls, beets, chef's salad, ice cream, cake, cookies, and more. When I saw the food his wife laid out on the table, it was as if I was beholding a vision of all the large billboard images of food I had pedaled hungrily by since Wisconsin. Sunday had been a hard and troubled day of riding, but at the end, what good fortune:

safe shelter and heaps of food. When the meal ended, tired and stuffed, I was ready to go back to the church and sleep.

Not yet. The Reverend had already made arrangements for us to go next door. Earlier I had mentioned to him that I had not seen television since I began my trip. So after supper, we went to the neighbor's home to watch TV. We watched a movie, *Cyrano de Bergerac*, a favorite play of mine at the time. Reverend West had never seen it before; he said he particularly liked the swordfight scenes.

When the movie was over, the minister would not consider letting me return to the church to sleep. He insisted I stay in their guest room. Reverend West, I thought, would probably be the most generous man I would meet on the trip.

I slept deeply and awoke refreshed, anxious to take my bike to the repair shop and be on my way. At breakfast, it became clear that the good Reverend was not through with me. He had noticed the severe sunburns on my hands and arms. He announced that we would get some salve for the burns. He had also decided that I needed a long-sleeved, light cotton shirt to protect my arms from the sun.

We dropped my bike off at the bike shop and went directly to a clothing store, where he purchased a shirt for me. Then we went on to a drugstore, where we found salve for my burns and suntan lotion. I protested at the expense Reverend West was going to. "It's all right," he replied. "I have a discretionary fund, you know." I was not the only one impressed with his generosity. "Is Bill a relative?" his friends would ask as he took me around town. "No, but we Episcopalians stick together like Jews," was his repeated reply. Finally, he dropped me off back at the bicycle shop to wait while the repairs were made.

The bicycle shop was really a motorcycle shop. When I brought my bike in that morning, the mechanic, who was also the owner, met me at the door. He was tall and heavy, with several days' growth of beard on his face. His hair was combed back on the sides, and he wore a brown leather jacket over a T-shirt. I showed him my problem, emphasized my lack of funds, and asked him to fix the bike if he could. I had only ten dollars in my pocket. He said he could fix it for $2.50. That was a bargain; I said okay.

I had been waiting only a short time at the bike shop when I saw the Reverend's station wagon return. He rolled his window down. "I called the editor of our newspaper," he said. "He wants a picture and a story. Hop in." In town we met a reporter from the *Daily Plainsman*. He asked about my plans for the rest of the trip, and I gave him answers as if I had a plan. The reporter wanted a photo of me with my bike. Reverend West told him we would be back when the bike was fixed.

After the interview, the Reverend stayed in town to pass the time while I walked back to the bike shop. When I arrived there, the repairs were finished. But according to the lady in the office, they had found more things wrong with the bike than expected. Dreading the news, I found the mechanic and asked him the price.

As he wiped the grease from his thick hands, the mechanic explained that the problem was not what he had thought. He had to replace some parts, and it had taken an hour and a half of his time. "How much will it be?" I asked, wondering hopelessly if I could eat on fifty cents a day. "Well," he replied, "as the poet said, 'A man should build his house by the side of the road and help his fellow man.' It's still $2.50." Such relief! As if suspended in a dream, I paid him, thanked him, and shook his hand.

We talked for a few minutes. He was attending night classes and hoped to be a history teacher one day. As we were talking, the Episcopalian minister's familiar station wagon wheeled into view again. He said he would give me a lift out of town to get me on my way, but first we needed to provide that photo the reporter wanted. With the bike loaded in his station wagon, we headed for the office of the *Daily Plainsman*. On the sidewalk in front of the office, I posed for a picture with my newly repaired bike.

Back in the car, we headed out of town. We

traveled about fifteen miles to a truck stop in a tiny town named Wolsey, where Reverend West intended to treat me to one last sandwich. We were unloading the bike when a truck driver, standing by the cab of a large grain elevator truck, yelled over that he was leaving immediately if I wanted a ride. I wheeled my bike over and loaded it into his truck.

When I looked back, Reverend West had disappeared. I climbed into the cab of the truck. Reverend West was still nowhere to be seen. As the driver put the truck into gear, the Reverend ran up to my window, pushing a roast beef sandwich at me. Walking along with the slowly rolling truck, he wished me luck, and I thanked him. On the move again, still eating, I took time to ponder the generous treatment I received in Huron, South Dakota, from my fellow Episcopalian and my fellow man.

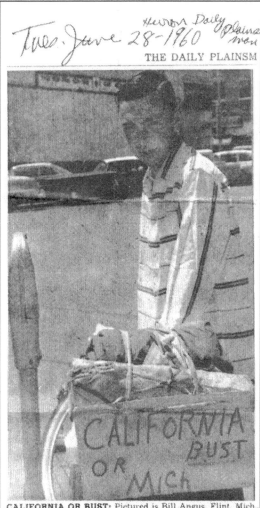

Tues. June 28-1960 *Huron Daily Plainsman*

THE DAILY PLAINSM

CALIFORNIA OR BUST: Pictured is Bill Angus, Flint, Mich., during his stop-over in Huron Monday afternoon. Bill hopes to reach San Francisco and return home before the last week in August.   (Daily Plainsman Photo)

On the following page is the article accompanying my photograph in the Daily Plainsman— regardless of the headline, I was not selling anything on the trip.

Michigan Youth Peddling To California

"California or Bust."

This sign appeared on the handle bars of a bicycle owned by Bill Angus, 19, son of Mr. and Mrs. Cecil J. Angus, Flint, Mich., Monday.

Bill had stopped to seek travel aid from Father Donald West at the Huron Episcopal Church Sunday night.

"The gear shift needed repairing. I came from Minneapolis in second gear, and thought I had better get it fixed here before I continued," he said.

His destination is San Francisco. However, he was careful to mention that because of a shortage of funds he might not complete his trip.

With $70 he had planned making the long journey in 65 days. His plans call for cycling most of the way there and getting rides back. He has until the last week in August, to do so.

"I won't make it in this time. I don't care if I fail to make it, but I wanted to try it just the same."

Saturday night was spent in the Brookings' jail.

"I didn't have enough money for a hotel room and it was getting late, so I asked for a cell."

Bill doesn't have a set route. He would like to travel from San Francisco down the coast of California and take pictures.

He left Flint June 17 and has averaged about 100 miles a day. He spent his 10th day in Huron.

"I'll never try this again," he said.

Catching Rides

Recall that the inspiration for this trip was a story I read at the age of thirteen about a youth who was given passage to Europe so that he might spend a month exploring the continent on a bicycle. I knew no one was going to pay for my passage across the Atlantic; therefore, in my imagination, California became my Europe. "California or Bust" read my sign. Unwittingly, however, I had changed the story. This was not to be my story about discovering California. It had become the story of my effort to pedal across an ocean of farmland and prairie.

I did not look for rides as I pedaled west, but I accepted them when offered. On my way through Minnesota, someone remarked that beyond Pierre, South Dakota, I would find the people much friendlier. If one construed that comment as referring specifically to the offer of rides—for sure a friendly gesture—then perhaps he was onto something. From the beginning of my trip on the shore of Lake Huron in Michigan, all the way until I reached South Dakota, I was offered one ride, which took me fifty miles out of my way. Once in South Dakota, however, even before I reached Pierre, kind folks were stopping to offer me a lift.

The driver of the grain elevator truck who picked me up in Wolsey took me eighty miles to Blunt, South Dakota. That put me within two hundred miles of Rapid City. Back on the bike, pedaling out of Blunt headed for Pierre—a distance of about twenty miles—I had barely covered five miles when a 1957 Chevy station wagon carrying four college girls stopped to offer me a ride. I could hardly say no. We had a serious struggle trying to force my bike into the back of the Chevy wagon, already loaded with their luggage. Finally, with one wheel sticking out of the back window, we took off. For the few minutes it took to reach Pierre, we talked about where I was from, what I was going to do in California, and whether I should even be accepting rides. The girls drove through Pierre and dropped me off on the west side of the Missouri River, in Fort Pierre.

It was about 5:00 in the afternoon when I waved goodbye to the Chevy full of girls. It was too early to stop for the day, so I spent seventy cents on a sandwich in a small café and resumed pedaling west on Route 14. I had gone no more than a mile when a family from St. Croix, Wisconsin, pulling a camper trailer, stopped to offer me a lift. We put the bike in the trailer, and they took me as far as Philip Junction, about ninety-three miles.

I pedaled on another seventeen miles. Darkness was settling when I came upon a roadside rest area. I pulled two picnic tables together, rolled out my sleeping bag on top of the tables, and went to sleep. On my tenth day—June 27—I had covered 226 miles, only twenty-five of them by bike.

The next morning I pedaled fifteen miles to Wall, South Dakota. Normally I would have pedaled on past a small town this early in the day, but I had been seeing the roadside signs since Minnesota: "Wall Drugs 465 miles," "Wall Drugs 375 miles," "Wall Drugs 212 miles." You get the idea. On this morning, as I entered Wall, a sign informed me that Wall Drugs was one mile further. I turned up Main Street to find this storied pharmacy. I found it waiting for me, like all the signs promised, and full of tourist trophies.

Back on Route 14, about five miles beyond Wall, my back tire went flat. After repairing it, I rode on to Wasta, where two young guys my own age offered me a ride to Rapid City. I reached Rapid City by 9:30 a.m. on June 28, a day earlier than I had anticipated.

Once in Rapid City, I headed directly for the

post office. It turned out that my parents had wasted no time getting a letter in the mail, and the postal service came through like champs. The letter awaited me in general delivery. Excited, I opened my first letter from home, and thankfully it included forty dollars. I rode to the public library so that I could finish the letter I was currently writing while comfortably seated at a library table, not, as usual, while sitting on the ground or on some random sidewalk bench.

Most days I would take time to write a few paragraphs to my folks, recounting recent highlights and experiences. Every two or three days I would finish a letter and mail it home. Now, sitting at a table in the Rapid City Library, I finished a letter that I had started in Minnesota. It would fill my folks in on my stay in the Brookings jail, my adventures with Reverend West of Huron, and the rides that brought me to Rapid City a day early.

As I was writing my letter, I was unaware that a part-time worker at the local TV station, KOTA, had noticed my bike with its "California or Bust" sign parked outside the library. He called the TV station, and a reporter came to the library and found me working on my letter. She interviewed me about the trip, took my picture and a picture of the bike, and told me I'd be on the 9:30 p.m. TV newscast in Rapid City. But I didn't wait around till 9:30 p.m. to see myself on TV. I finished my letter, posted it, and got ready to head west to the Black Hills National Forest.

A few days before, when I had made the decision to stop for a day or two of rest in the Black Hills, I had looked on my map and identified two campgrounds where I could stay: the Rockerville Campground, about twelve miles beyond Rapid City, and the Stockade Lake Campground, a little further on in Custer. Before leaving Rapid City, I wrote a postcard to Al identifying both campgrounds and left it in care of general delivery at the post office.

I pedaled out of Rapid City around midday. On most other days, I would pedal twelve to fifteen hours and then, as evening settled in, feel my anxiety rise as I began to look for a safe place to sleep. This day, I knew I would spend the night at the Rockerville Campground, just twelve miles ahead. I felt relaxed.

I reached the campground by midafternoon and set up a campsite among a stand of pine trees on a rocky rise. I enjoyed the restful afternoon and the sense of satisfaction in having made it to the Black Hills. They had seemed so far away that first day in Wisconsin when I turned the corner on Highway 8 and headed west.

It began to drizzle. For the first time on the trip, I pitched my handmade pup tent. It was made of lightweight canvas that I had sewn together myself. Because I wanted it to be as small and light as possible, and therefore easier to pack, it was just slightly more than half the width and height of a normal pup tent. Once I crawled inside this pint-sized tent, if I moved at all, I could not help but touch the canvas; and wherever I touched the tent's canvas sides, water would drip through. The eleventh day was over; it rained most of the night.

The Black Hills, enough said.

I stayed at the Rockerville Campground all day Wednesday, resting and eating. On the back of an envelope I added up the miles I had come from Flint to Rapid City. By my calculation, I had covered 1,361 miles. The thought of turning around and heading home didn't offer relief now; home was as far away as California. And the hope of meeting up with my friend Al still lingered. I spent a second night at Rockerville and waited by my campsite until 1:00 in the afternoon on Thursday, on the faint hope that a yellow Dodge would roll into view. It didn't. I packed my gear and headed out to see Mt. Rushmore on my way to the Stockade Lake Campground near Custer, a small town about twenty-five miles beyond Rockerville.

The Black Hills were beautiful. The road wound around ridges and offered views of streams below and wooded hillsides above. The approach to Mt. Rushmore was a two-mile uphill ride on a narrow, winding side road. In 1960, the monument was not the developed tourist site it is today. It was a rustic park with a lookout from which visitors could gaze on the faces of the four presidents. It was a moving experience to ride up through the pine forest to behold that monumental mountainside sculpture. I followed a hiking trail a short way on my bike, taking in the view for a few minutes, before I turned around and coasted back to the highway and headed toward my next campground in Custer.

Mt Rushmore, 1960.

On a map of the Black Hills, I noticed what looked like a side road that would shave a few miles off the ride. I took it. I pedaled along, enjoying the scenery, until I came to a sign that read, "Buffalo area, stay in your car." There were no precautions offered for bicyclists. Can a highly motivated cyclist pedal faster than a buffalo can run? I proceeded on. Fortunately, I saw no buffalo

on the way to Custer, and not for lack of looking. I made it safely through the buffalo area and
found the Stockade Lake Campground.

The camp at Stockade Lake was in a scenic
setting. I met a family there who lived in Penn-
sylvania, but the wife was originally from Flint.
They gave me a roast beef dinner and a breakfast.
They said sometime when they were in Flint they
would stop in. I added that story to my next letter
home, which I had begun writing at Rockerville.

After leaving the Stockade Lake Campground
Friday afternoon, I stopped briefly in Custer.
While there, another newspaper reporter asked
me for an interview. Her brief article, accompanied by a photograph of me standing by my bike,
appeared in the Custer County Chronicle almost a
week later, on July 7. It read as follows:

Bill Angus, a 19-year old college student
from Flint, Mich., rode through Custer July 1
on the bicycle he is riding from Flint Mich.,
to San Francisco. Bill camped at Stockade
Lake last Thursday night and passed through
Custer Friday. He had his camping and cooking equipment on the back of his bicycle.

Angus stated that he is not trying to set
any kind of cross-country record; he is making the trip for his own enjoyment. Bill has
been averaging about 100 miles a day, and if
time permits, he will ride his bicycle back to
Michigan in time to re-enter College this fall.

I told my parents about the interview in my letter:

> *I got my picture in another paper, the one in Custer. You should get a copy soon. I saw the article from the Plainsman and I didn't like it. When he interviewed me he took no direct quotes, yet he credited me with them. I hope you did not get the wrong impression from that bit about "never doing it again." Of course I won't. I never imagined that I would do it again. But it is not as bad as all that.*

Photo retrieved from the microfilm archives of the Custer County Chronicle.

That *Reader's Digest* article I read in the ninth grade, the article that planted the seed for this trip, seemed to have stirred to life in South Dakota. The article extolled the value of travelling to unfamiliar places as a young person—not only as a means of discovering the humanity of people but, through these adventures, discovering one's own strengths. South Dakota had been such an experience. From my first day in the state—when my bike broke down as I approached Huron under the threat of a tornado warning and Reverend West, and then the bike mechanic, befriended me—to the kindness of people, both east and west of Pierre, who offered me rides and sped me across the hot and arid plains, giving me time to rest for a couple of days in the Black Hills, South Dakota had embraced this traveler. I had been written up in two newspapers, with accompanying photos, and interviewed by a TV news reporter.

Also important was what did not happen in South Dakota. I did not catch a ride with my friend Al in his yellow Dodge. I had hoped, especially in that difficult first week, that he and I would meet up somewhere—perhaps near Rapid City, as we had discussed the morning I left Huron Beach—and that I might catch a ride with him, maybe all the way to the coast. Now, as I headed west into Wyoming, the idea of catching a ride with Al was behind me. I did not feel disappointed or anxious. A lot had changed in two weeks of riding. I was halfway to California. I was rested. I knew I could make it.

With Custer behind me, I rode west on Highway 16 another thirty-five miles, crossed into Wyoming, and arrived at the junction of Highways 16 and 85 about 6:00 in the evening. I turned south on Highway 85, intending to make another thirty miles before dark. I found the Wyoming countryside even more desolate than South Dakota. I rode for miles without seeing a house. Then my rear tire blew out. The tire itself had ruptured. I had already used my spare, and I could not repair the flat. I sat beside the road, in the middle of nowhere, and waited.

In about ten minutes, a pickup truck came along. I stuck my thumb out. The pickup stopped. The driver said he was going to Denver. I rode 222 miles with him, into the dark night, to Cheyenne, Wyoming, where he dropped me off after midnight.

I went to a police station. They had no available jail cell, but they let me sleep on a bench in the back of a courtroom. The officer who led me to the courtroom mumbled some remark, seemingly not addressed to me directly, about vagrants. That was the first rudeness I had encountered on the trip. I rolled out my sleeping bag on a bench in the back of the court room and fell asleep.

In the morning I located a bicycle shop. While waiting for it to open, I finished writing my letter home. I had to replace the tire and tube as well as a spoke. It cost $4.95. I was back on the road by 9:30 that morning, Saturday, July 2.

The Lincoln Highway

The road I would follow across Wyoming was first dedicated as the Lincoln Highway in 1913. The original Lincoln Highway started at Times Square in New York City and ended at Lincoln Park in San Francisco. In the mid-1920s the federal government began numbering highways, and the Lincoln Highway became US 30. It was a primary coast-to-coast route until the era of interstate expressways in the 1960s.

On the west side of Wyoming, at the time of my ride, US 30 split into 30 South and 30 North. US 30 South followed the original Lincoln Highway route to San Francisco; US 30 North went up through Idaho and Oregon, finally reaching the Pacific coast at Astoria, Oregon. I planned to follow the southern route to California. Today most of old US 30 has been replaced with Interstate 80, which does not follow, exactly, the old US 30 route I bicycled in 1960.

As I left Cheyenne, my objective for my first day in Wyoming seemed modest: get past Laramie. Laramie was only fifty miles west of Cheyenne, but ever since Minnesota, people had been warning me about a forty-mile-long hill between Cheyenne and Laramie. The Continental Divide runs roughly north to south through Wyoming, passing near Laramie. Most of my ride to Laramie would be a steady ascent of about two thousand feet up the eastern slope of the Laramie Mountains to the summit of Sherman Hill at an elevation of 8,835 feet. That morning there was no headwind, so the ride, even though it was a long, uphill grind, was not bad. It would take me five hours to reach Laramie.

As I worked my way up that long hill, I occasionally stopped to rest. At one point near Sherman Summit I came upon a combination gas station and sandwich shop, a tourist oasis sprawled along the empty roadside. I hungered for a real sandwich, so I decided to splurge. Instead of making another peanut butter and jelly lunch by the side of the road, I went into the shop, ordered a chicken sandwich, and took it back outside. I stood in the shade of an awning, straddling my bike while I ate.

Suddenly a man appeared beside me. Extending his hand to offer me a dollar bill, he said, "It's not much, but I hope it will help." Not knowing what to say, I accepted the dollar bill and thanked him. Without another word, he turned and walked to an Oldsmobile sedan parked at the gas pumps, got in, and drove away. I was surprised, but I assumed that the "California or Bust" sign still tied to the back of my bike had prompted his generosity. I finished my sandwich, got back up on the seat of my bike, and headed for Laramie.

The small western cities I passed though in 1960 seemed odd to me. As I approached a city, it looked ordinary enough at first, similar to the peripheries of the small cities I was familiar with in Michigan. Back home, as one approached a city he or she would pass through a commercial stretch with an assortment of separate one and two-story buildings. Reaching the center of the city one would find a few blocks of taller office buildings, a couple of department stores, and perhaps apartment buildings. Out west, the assortment of separate commercial buildings would appear for a few miles, then fade away, and I would be back in the empty plains. The center of the city was missing. That was Laramie in 1960.

By midafternoon I was west of Laramie. The long climb up the eastern slope of the Laramie Mountains was behind me, so I decided to keep riding. The wind had picked up out of the west, the usual headwind. The land was as desolate as ever—miles went by, but nothing changed. There were no houses, no fences, no trees, just the empty plains. Was I even moving?

One memorable moment did occur in the course of this endless emptiness. It was something that happened nowhere else on the trip: I met another cross-country bicyclist. He was resting beside the road, so I stopped to talk to him. He had a dark red, three-speed English bike similar to my own and loaded with gear. For a few minutes, resting in Wyoming, we talked about where we were from, where we were going, and our bicycling experiences. He looked to be in his mid twenties. The difference in the way we had approached our respective cross-country adventures was obvious: direction. He was pedaling from the Pacific coast to his home in Indiana. He had planned to take advantage of the prevailing westerly wind by putting it at his back. He was a bicyclist. I was just a kid on an adventure, searching for California.

The fact that I encountered only one cross-country bicyclist in 1960 is not surprising. Once automobiles became popular in the United States, bicycle use by adults declined sharply. Bicycles became children's toys. Recall that it was a thirteen-year-old ninth grader in 1954 who dreamed up the idea for this trip. It wasn't until the 1960s that a revival of adult interest in bicycling began to develop, mainly as a fitness exercise. That's when the English three-speed became a trendy bike. By the 1980s, mountain biking and recreational touring by bike had become popular. But in 1960, cross-country bicycling was unusual in the United States.

I pedaled on until dusk settled on the empty prairie. Before the interstate expressway system was built, US 30 was a primary cross-country highway. This meant I had to share my half of US 30 with plenty of trucks. I tried riding into the night, because the headwinds died down in the evening. But the truck traffic increased at night, and sharing a two-lane road after dark with speeding tractor-trailer trucks was scary. On the plus side, sleeping accommodations were everywhere, since there wasn't a building within miles and not a fence anywhere. I could simply steer my bike out into the prairie forty or fifty yards and rolled out my sleeping bag. It was that simple. I didn't have to search for the most comfortable, most private, or safest spot, because there was only one spot as far as the eye could see, as long as I didn't lie down on U.S 30 itself.

As I pedaled toward Wyoming, another feature of the western plains that folks offering travel advice would often mention was that if you sleep on the ground out here on the western plain, snakes will occasionally snuggle up next to you for warmth. Rattlesnakes were common on the high plains and, I was told, would sometimes slide right into your sleeping bag with you. But that night, I wasn't stopping at the Hotel High Plains for the amenities. I was stopping because I needed sleep, snakes or no snakes.

I laid my bike down, rolled out my sleeping bag, and prepared to crawl in. When I took my pants off, I saw what must have motivated the driver of the Olds parked behind me at that gas station and sandwich shop east of Laramie to give me the dollar. His words were, "It's not much, but I hope it will help." The seat of my pants was completely gone, worn away by the seat of the bicycle. Now I recalled the muttered slur—"vagrant"—uttered by the deputy at the Cheyenne police station the previous night. I didn't lose any sleep over this, and perhaps it was my shabby attire that kept the snakes at a distance. Anyway, I had another pair of pants, so when I left the next morning I was rested and properly dressed.

I was back on the road by 6:00 Sunday morning, and the wind was behind me. I made good time. I passed through Medicine Bow by 8:30. I rode a little way beyond the town and pulled off the road to enjoy another peanut butter and jelly sandwich.

As I ate, I was considering the advice offered by the driver of that grain elevator truck back in South Dakota. He said that Wyoming, Utah, and Nevada were so arid and vacant that I should look for truck rides to cover some of those miles. As I was weighing this possibility, a truck passed by. I didn't pay attention to it until I noticed that it had stopped about a hundred yards up the road and was turning around. The small red box truck approached and slowed to a stop. The driver rolled down his window and asked if I was going west. He said he was on his way to Portland, Oregon, and would be glad to give me a ride. I thanked him but explained that I was headed to California. Not satisfied with my response, he explained that he could at least give me a lift to the fork in US 30 where US 30 North splits off and goes north to Oregon. That would be a ride of about two hundred miles. I accepted.

I hoisted my bike into the back of the empty truck and climbed into the cab. The driver explained that he was taking the truck back to Portland after it had been used on a rental trip. For much of the next hour, he described the difficulty he thought I would have bicycling across the Nevada desert: I would have to travel at night because the days were too hot, and I might encounter unsavory inhabitants out in the desert. The heat and desert dwellers aside, he argued that a ride down the Pacific coast from Portland to San Francisco would be far more interesting and spectacular than pedaling across the Nevada desert. His argument was starting to make sense.

One aspect of my plan that still needed to be fleshed out was my destination. Although the Lincoln Highway ended in San Francisco, in my

mind my destination was still nothing more specific than "California." My mother, however, had
a Canadian cousin who owned a farm in Riverside, California. This was a relative whom I had
never met. She wrote to her cousin, Tyler Cowan,
to advise him that her only child, whom he didn't
know from Adam, might be arriving at his door
soon, hungry and looking for work. Therefore, it
is fair to say that Riverside, California was one
possible destination.

The route down the Pacific coast from Portland
to San Francisco was approximately four hundred
miles shorter than the trek from Medicine Bow to
San Francisco. That would save me perhaps four
days—enough time to travel from San Francisco
on to Riverside, if I could not find work in the city
by the sea. Riding along in the cab of this truck,
my plan was coming into focus, as they say, in
real time. I accepted the truck driver's offer of a
ride to Portland.

I soon understood why the driver wanted company. He loved to talk. I heard one story after
another over the next two days. We followed US
30 west and then north across the plains of south-
western Wyoming and southern Idaho and then
into Oregon. I found the western plains more
enjoyable at fifty-five and sixty miles per hour.
It was a fine ride, all against a backdrop of the
driver's countless stories—many of them about
the women he had known, in the biblical sense.

At the end of the day we were well into Idaho. We stopped for the night in a pullout beside the highway, crawled into the back of the empty truck, rolled out our sleeping bags, and slept.

The next morning, before we left, I climbed a steep hill across the road and took a picture looking down on the small red box truck that plucked me out of Medicine Bow, Wyoming, and would drop me off in Portland, Oregon.

By the time we were back on the road, the crows and vultures were well on with their task of cleaning the "table"— US 30— of the previous night's roadkill. By midday we had crossed into Oregon. Through both Wyoming and Oregon, US 30 North roughly followed the old Oregon

Trail, forged by fur trappers and later, in the mid-nineteenth century, by westward-bound settlers. Between Baker City and Pendleton, Oregon, we came into the Blue Mountains. They were a spectacular sight to a boy from Michigan. According to my driver and guide, the Blue Mountains were the last major barrier faced by settlers following the Oregon Trail on their way to eastern Washington or to the Willamette Valley in western Oregon. We reached the Columbia River at Boardman, Oregon. From there we followed the Colombia River to Portland, enjoying the mountain scenery and the beauty of the Columbia River Valley.

One of our take-in-the-scenery stops along the
Columbia River.

By definition, one does not anticipate the events of an unplanned journey; but when the journey is done one has the memories. I have memories of following the historic Oregon Trail to the Columbia River and enjoying the spectacular views of the Columbia River Valley all the way to Portland. For those memories, I thank the driver of that red box truck, who spared me a ride across the Nevada desert and regaled me with two days of storytelling. He dropped me off in Portland on a street corner near the west bank of the Willamette River. After days on the prairie and the plains, Portland seemed crowded and dense with people and buildings. It was too late in the evening to bicycle out of the city and search for a campsite. Over the previous three nights I had slept on a courtroom bench in Cheyenne, under the stars on the plains west of Laramie, and in the back of a parked truck in Idaho. Now, here in the city of Portland, I chose the YMCA.

Coasting

It was Tuesday, July 5. I checked out of the Portland YMCA and began a ninety-mile ride to Lincoln City, Oregon, on the Pacific coast, relieved to be done with the arid plains, the constant headwinds, and the prospect of spending days in the desert heat. I found my way across Portland and took Highway 99 west to McMinnville. There I turned onto Highway 18, which followed the Salmon River toward the coast. Through the pine trees, I could often see the water sparkling as it rippled over the rocks on its own gentle descent to the Pacific. By early evening I had reached the coast and turned south on Highway 101.

To a teenage boy from the Midwest in 1960, one who had spent most of his high school years reading hot rod magazines and tinkering with cars, Highway 101 was mythic. The first sanctioned drag race in California happened on a service drive off Highway 101 north of Santa Barbara in 1949. Now that I was a college student, hot-rodding was behind me, but it was a thrill to be riding on Highway 101.

I rode through Lincoln City and continued south, eventually stopping for the night at a state campground. I checked in at the camp entrance and then pedaled into the park to find my camp-site. I found it at the foot of a giant redwood tree—the first redwood I had ever seen up close. The trunk must have been eight feet in diameter. The tree towered into the sky. I ate, then rolled out my sleeping bag under this redwood giant and fell asleep.

I had finally reached the Pacific. I had seen my first redwood trees. One might have expected a cross-country traveler to stop here for a day, to sit on the shore of the ocean, admire the beauty of the redwoods, enjoy a sense of accomplishment, and rest. Instead, as I did every other morning, I awoke early and got back on the road. Each day had the same agenda: start early and keep going until dusk. As I pedaled out of the campground that morning, fog shrouded the trees and two elk grazed at the edge of the forest.

The mountains in the Pacific Coast Range fol-low the coastline from Canada through California. The Oregon Coast Highway, Highway 101, cuts a path south between the Oregon Coast Range and the shore of the Pacific Ocean. As the geog-raphy would suggest, much of the Oregon Coast Highway is an up and down ride. I would spend grueling hours pedaling uphill in first or second gear. Then the good part would come: coasting downhill. On a steep downhill slope, I could often keep up with the cars, since they had to reduce their speed to maintain control around the sharp curves. In one long stretch of modestly downward sloping highway, I coasted most of the time for four hours. The Oregon coastline is beautiful, but I was not into the scenery. I was weary and single-mindedly focused on reaching San Francisco. Eventually another long day ended, and I settled down to sleep in another state campground on the coast.

The next morning I was back on the road by 8:00. The mornings were cool along the coast, and I soon realized I had left my jacket back at the campground. I returned to my campsite but could not find the jacket. I asked at the park office if it had been turned in. It had not. A worker in the office went out to ask another park ranger if he had found the coat. While I waited, I added a few lines to another letter home.

Friday, July 7

The weather is very cold at night by the ocean and I have lost my jacket. Some park workers are looking for it. I hope they find it. A scoutmaster who camped next to me last night treated me to a pancake breakfast this morning. He used a good mix that you only have to add wa-

ter to cook. I hope to have some hot meals now. Everyone here tells me California will be a disappointment. That is, they say there is not anything special to see and the people are not very friendly because there are so many travelers and migrants there all the time. The park staff could not find my coat. Well, I haven't made very much time so far today. Let me know how everyone is at home. How is Dad's job hanging on? And Boots? I will write again soon.

Love, Bill

Boots was my childhood dog, given to me as a pup. Her health had been declining rapidly. The letter I had received from my folks when I was in Rapid City brought news that she might be gone before I returned home. As for my dad's job, he was a trade union millwright. Like most trade union workers in Michigan, when the automobile companies were adding capacity or undergoing a model changeover, he had work; when the economy was slow, there was little or no work. Millwright work had been infrequent in 1958 and 1959, so those were difficult years for my parents. By the summer of 1960, however, work had started to pick up, and Dad was even getting overtime. I hoped the good news about his job would continue.

I later learned that my letters home had, as we would say today, gone viral—at least in Flushing.

Mother had been reading them to her friends, one of whom volunteered to type them up "for future reference." She proceeded to type two copies: one for Mother to give to me when I returned, and one to pass around among friends and neighbors. As a result, the story of my trip was being widely shared around town. Even one of my former high school teachers was discussing my bicycle trip in a summer school class.

After finishing my letter, I left the park jacketless, and off to a late start. My problems, however, were put into perspective a few hours later when I met an entire family of hungry travelers. I had stopped at a small lookout to rest and have a bite to eat when an old pickup truck pulled in and parked. It had a topper over the bed. The driver got out and approached me. He asked if I had any milk. He was Mexican, a migratory farm worker. His child needed the milk, he explained. I offered him the only milk I had, half a box of powdered milk. He took it and introduced me to his wife and child, who were huddled in the back of the truck. That was where he and his family lived. They had been in Oregon looking for work and now were headed back to California. After a few minutes of conversation we both returned to the road and our separate journeys. A couple more hours of pedaling along the coast and I came to another campground where I would spend my last night in Oregon.

I crossed into California in the late afternoon of July 8. Once in California, Highway 101 moved away from the coast, the land became flatter, and the countryside was dotted with homes, commercial buildings, and crossroads. The area was too settled to just roll out a sleeping bag by the side of the road. I began to worry that finding a nearby campsite for the night would be difficult. The trip was beginning to tell on me. I had been on the road for three weeks now, pedaling from early morning to sunset on most days and eating poorly.

About 7:00 in the evening I stopped at a small store to purchase pancake mix and more powdered milk. I asked the clerk how far it was to the next campground. He estimated forty-five miles. I was disheartened. I could not pedal another forty-five miles that day.

I rode on, uncertain of what to do. I pedaled about two miles down the road, the last stretch up a gradual rise. As I passed over the crest of the rise and looked ahead, to my great relief I saw a small roadside park with perhaps twenty campsites. It was not a normal campground. The park had no caretaker, no electricity, no showers, and no fee, but to this weary rider it was an oasis, a gift. Perhaps it existed especially for the peripatetic—the migrant laborers and the occasional wandering bicyclist.

Only two other campers were in the park. The

ground in the campsite was sandy; it felt like beach sand underfoot. I sat down to rest and took off my shoes before setting about to gather sticks for a fire so I could cook pancakes.

I went to a public faucet near the center of the park to get water. As I walked back, with each step my bare feet sank into the soft, warm, embracing sand. I felt safe and so thankful to have found a quite, peaceful place to rest. Then, startled, I heard my own voice speak aloud the words, "Thank you, Lord." They were not my words, but I spoke them. I was stunned. At seventeen I had declared myself done with religion. Now, two years later, I heard my own voice thanking the Lord for bringing me to this campsite, this safe haven.

I kept on walking across the warm sand, laced with tufts of grass, back to my campsite and my pancakes. The pancakes were wonderful, and I slept well. I would be in San Francisco in three days.

Early the next morning I was back on my bike, heading south on Highway 101. Late in the morning, somewhere between Crescent City and Eureka, I stopped at a scenic roadside pullout to take a break. A few minutes later, an old black Buick sedan wheeled into the pullout, and three young guys climbed out of the front seat. Now that I was in California the sign still hanging on the back of my bike—"California or Bust, Mich."—started a different conversation. There was no advice about the trip ahead, the difficulty of the uphill climb to the Continental Divide in Wyoming, or the hot and dangerous Nevada desert. The questions now were about the story of the ride: How long did it take to get here? What route did I follow? And the big one: What did I plan to do now that I had reached California?

The first thing I was going to do, I told these three who had just sprung from the Buick, was look up a friend. The letter I had received from my folks in Rapid City included the address of Doug Deneen, a friend from high school who had joined the navy. He was now stationed near San Francisco and was living off base with his sister and her husband in San Rafael, just north of San Francisco. His sister's address was my destination now. The Buick three immediately offered me a ride. They were on their way to San Francisco and would be passing right through San Rafael.

A ride in that old Buick didn't seem plausible; the back seat was stuffed to the roof with their luggage, and the three of them were riding in the front seat. And what about the bike? No problem. They proceeded to mount the bike on the rear bumper and tie it with rope to the rear door handles. After they finished, I took a picture. One guy was seated on the bike and the other two were sitting on the Buick's roof.

Four in the front seat to San Rafael.

We were ready to go. The four of us all slid into the front seat, with the understanding that should we see a police car, one of us (but not the driver) would have to slide down below the window, since four in the front seat was not legal in California.

The ride was uneventful, except for a stop at the Swiss Colony winery in Asti, where we pulled in to sample the wine. I mailed a free postcard home from the winery, postage included, courtesy of Swiss Colony. The guys dropped me off in San Rafael in the late afternoon, and I set about trying to find Doug Deneen's sister's apartment.

San Rafael is a hilly town. Eventually I found the place at the top of a long, steep hill: a large three-story house split up into several apartments.

Doug's sister's apartment was at the top, three flights up a set of outside stairs as steep as the hill I had just pedaled up. Although this certainly looked like a modest apartment building, the view from the top of the stairs was spectacular.

I knocked on the door. No one answered, so I went back down the stairs. Across the street stood a single-car garage, its door open, revealing an early fifties Chevy with Michigan plates parked inside. I rolled my bike into the garage and tried the car door. It wasn't locked. I got in the car and lay down in the front seat to wait for someone to come back. I fell asleep.

Suddenly I heard a man's loud voice. "Get out of this car! Come on!" I opened my eyes. It was dark, except for a flashlight aimed at me. I could make out two figures, one behind the other. The one in front was holding a revolver. I was looking directly into the muzzle. I could see bullets in the chambers of the cylinder. The light from the flashlight reflected on a man's face—the face I was waiting for. "Is that you, Doug?" I asked. "It's me, Bill." He recognized me and put the gun down.

Doug's sister and her husband were very welcoming, and I spent two days with them in San Rafael. In the San Francisco phone directory, I found the address and phone number of Conard House, which at the time was the headquarters for the San Francisco chapter of the Youth Hostel Association. I made arrangements for a week's lodging. On the morning of Monday, July 11, Doug drove me into San Francisco, across the Golden Gate Bridge, to 2441 Jackson Street, the youth hostel I had been hoping to find since leaving Minneapolis. I thanked Doug and said goodbye to my high school friend. It was the last time our paths would cross.

Lost in San Francisco

The youth hostel was a weary-looking, three-story Victorian row house on Jackson Street, just west of Fillmore Street in the Pacific Heights neighborhood. Steps rose sharply from the sidewalk to a porch supporting two ornate pillars. Between the pillars hung a sign lettered in what looked like a comic font, identifying the old Victorian as "CONARD HOUSE." A row of windows across the front of the house looked down on Jackson Street. The steps led up to a pair of tall, ornate front doors with inlaid stained glass. As boarding houses go, it was elegant, if old and worn.

Stepping through the front door into the entrance hall, I found myself in a sea of woodwork punctuated with stained glass windows and faded wallpaper. A sign directed me up dimly lit stairs to an office located at the back of the third floor. The small room was filled with sunlight from a

The Conard House on Jackson Ave. Seated on the steps is Joe, one of my two roommates from New York. Standing is Roy Nimmons from Belfast, Ireland.

curtainless window. There I found the proprietress, a woman who looked to be about forty. Her name was Elaine, and she ran the boarding house with the help of an assistant, a younger woman named Joan. They both lived on the third floor. The rate was ten dollars per week.

After I checked in, Joan showed me to a room on the second floor. The room was dimly lit. The wallpaper had been painted over, perhaps to make it appear less Victorian and a little brighter. The room had three metal-framed beds, a table and chairs. She explained I would be sharing the room with two guys from New York. She then took me to the back of the old Victorian, where there was an entrance to a small utility room in the basement, a space to store my bike. The basement level included a communal kitchen with two refrigerators, where residents could store and prepare their own food. Next to the kitchen, a community room with sofas, chairs, a ping-pong table, and a TV gave residents a place to meet. Joan, my guide to Conard House, told me that once a week, movies were shown in this room.

As soon as I had moved my belongings to my room, I started looking for work. I searched the want ads and asked around, but to no avail. A clerk working at the employment office told me there were five college students for every summer job in San Francisco. I figured I would run out of money in about a week, and it looked like it might take more than a week to find a job, if I could find one at all. I had fifty dollars left in a savings account at home. That afternoon, facing the possibility that I might not find work before I ran out of money, I airmailed a letter home, asking my folks to wire me the fifty dollars as quickly as possible.

Because I was so preoccupied with the need to find work, I do not have many clear memories of my first look at the city. I did find a market on the corner of Fillmore and Jackson Streets where I could buy groceries. A little further up Jackson Street, to the west, I found Alta Plaza Park, with its splendid view of San Francisco to the south and southeast and San Francisco Bay and Alcatraz

Island to the north. I have a clear image of standing in Alta Park that first afternoon, looking out over the rooftops of San Francisco and embracing the vision of that beautiful city. The vivid image has never faded from my memory. It was more than the beauty of the city that impressed the moment in my mind; it was also an awareness, which I had not yet given words to, that I had reached my destination. For that moment, I forgot about having no money, needing work, and not knowing what the next day would bring.

Like roads, hostels are full of travelers. All the boarders may not have been travelers, but they all were young. My roommates were two young black guys from New York. It was the summer of 1960, less than a year before the first Freedom Rides to Alabama and Mississippi; but this was San Francisco, and the three of us seemed to be comfortable with each other. The older roommate, Joe, looked to be in his late twenties; the younger one, Michael, was only a little older than me. They had been in the city two weeks, looking for work.

The hostel was also a temporary home for three guys from Seattle who were on their way to Mexico by car, and students from other parts of California who were visiting San Francisco. And there was one traveler whose ambition and

Roy Nimmons on his borrowed bike.

A cable car on California St. near Stockton St.

imagination outdistanced us all. He was a lad about my age from Belfast, Ireland. His name was Roy Nimmons, and he was on his way around the world. He had hitchhiked across the United States to reach San Francisco. Roy and I arrived at Conard House at about the same time, and we hit it off, swapping stories about hitchhiking versus bicycling cross-country.

Neither of us had yet done much sightseeing, Somehow Roy came up with a bike—a girl's bike that I believe the proprietress loaned to him. We spent much of the next three days—Tuesday, Wednesday and Thursday— exploring the city and taking in the sights. Touring San Francisco by bicycle had its up and downs—and steep ones—but the views were spectacular. We bicycled through the Pacific Heights neighborhood, down streets lined with rows of old Victorian houses, and to Alta Park. We bicycled down Jackson Street to Chinatown and over to Market Street. We rode on the trolley cars. I was left with an impression of San Francisco as an exotic mix of cultures more vivid than anything I had seen before.

For me, San Francisco just happened to be the city at the end of the road to California, a joyful surprise after a long, grueling ride. Roy came for a specific reason: he hoped to find passage on a freighter bound out of the Port of San Francisco to his next destination, Australia. His plan was to get a job on a freighter and work off his passage. He attempted to persuade me to go with him. Finding work on an ocean-going freighter sounded intriguing to me. So each morning we biked down to the docks to inquire about freighters headed for Australia. Nothing turned up, but we came back each day to ask again.

Although race never emerged as an issue between me and my roommates, the younger one, Michael, was more distant and a little edgy with Roy. At one point Michael, Roy, and I were in the kitchen, each making our own lunch fare, when Roy complained about some foreign matter in the jar of mayonnaise. Michael seemed to take offense at the word "foreign" and asked Roy what he meant. Roy replied that the mayonnaise wasn't pure. A moment of tense silence followed. Then it passed. Michael seemed to decide that Roy wasn't making racial allusions, that he was a foreigner who probably did not understand the layered connotations words have in America when passed across racial lines.

That day in the kitchen was Wednesday, July 13, 1960. In Los Angeles, at the Democratic National Convention, John F. Kennedy was nominated to be the party's presidential candidate. We watched the news on the TV set in the community room—or, as the proprietress referred to it, the rumpus room.

Of my two roommates, Joe was the friendlier. He said he was a photographer hoping to find work in San Francisco. I never saw any camera equipment; perhaps he was working mostly with hope. He appeared to be having some luck with Joan, the hostel manager's assistant, a white girl who tended to work the office counter in her slip. The two of them would go out most evenings. They would ask me to come with them down to North Beach. But I wanted to see San Francisco, not sit in a bar and drink.

It wasn't until four years later, as I lay in my army bunk reading *The Subterraneans* by Jack Kerouac, that I realized what I had missed. There I was in San Francisco in 1960, and a black roommate from New York and a local girl were inviting me to go with them to visit some North Beach bars—the very bars that may have been the haunts of Allen Ginsberg or Lawrence Ferlinghetti or even Jack Kerouac on his visits to the city. But I had not yet read these writers, even though I may have been searching for them. The San Francisco of 1960 offered me a foreign land I could have been exploring, but I was unaware of that San Francisco. I was watching the trolley cars, visiting Chinatown, and taking in the sights.

A favorite spot of mine in Conard House was, a window seat in the foyer or entrance hall. When you descended the main staircase from the second or third floors to the main floor you would find yourself in the foyer. To me, this entry hall seemed stately—a high-ceilinged, formal space with an abundance of woodwork and faded wallpaper. Light in the foyer was subdued, mainly filtering through the large window to the left of the front door. The window framed a view of Jackson Street from seven or eight feet above street level. I enjoyed sitting on the window seat in that stately old foyer, watching people walk up and down the street, wondering who they were and where they were going.

On Thursday the proprietress, Elaine, decided to visit a friend in Sausalito. Joan and Joe were also going. Whether it was their idea or Elaine's I do not know, but Roy and I were invited to join them. I had never heard of Sausalito, which in 1960 was a small artists' colony with a Bohemian flavor, but I accepted the invitation. We all climbed into Elaine's convertible and drove across the Golden Gate Bridge.

Elaine's friend and our host, Sam, had a home with a view of San Francisco Bay. We spent a few hours on the lawn, talking and admiring the view. It included one anomaly. Anchored out in the bay were row after row of mothballed freighters—hundreds of freighters used in wartime, waiting to be of use again. These mothballed freighters were the only subject I focused the lens of my camera on during my visit to Sausalito. I did not take a photo of the host or his home, nor my friends, nor Elaine, who brought us—just the mothballed boats.

The mothball fleet in San Francisco Bay

Often we do not easily recognize, or take an interest in that which we do not already know or find familiar. I did not know Elaine. I later learned that Elaine Mikels was a social worker by training and had traveled extensively as a youth, thus explaining her involvement with youth hostels. She was a social worker in San Francisco in the 1950s when she acquired the old Victorian boarding house on Jackson Street. She named it Conard House, continuing to operate it as a boarding house and also, through her association with the American Youth Hostels organization, as a hostel. Even more remarkable, through Elaine's professional contacts in the San Francisco social work community, by 1960 Conard House had become a national model as a halfway house for young people transitioning out of mental institutions back into the community.

Decades later, I discovered that in 1986 Elaine wrote a memoir titled *Just Lucky I Guess: From Closet Lesbian to Radical Dike*. It's an interesting and thoughtful work about her experiences growing up as a lesbian in the 1940s and 1950s and becoming a lesbian activist in the 1960s. In her memoir, Elaine explained that she chose to live in San Francisco because she found that city's charms similar to those of the European and Middle Eastern cities she had visited in her youthful travels. She specifically related how the Italian neighborhood of North Beach and the artists' colony of Sausalito were welcoming and comfortable for gays and lesbians in the 1950s and 1960s. But I was unaware of all this on that July afternoon in 1960 Sausalito, standing in the yard of Elaine's friend, absorbed in the spectacle of mothballed freighters at anchor in San Francisco Bay.

On Thursday morning, before our visit to Sausalito, Roy and I had bicycled down to the docks to inquire again about ships bound for Australia. On this visit someone working on the docks advised us that we should go to Vancouver if we were serious about finding work on a freighter bound for Australia. Vancouver was a much bigger shipping port than San Francisco, and Canada, being in the

British Commonwealth, would have more business with Australia. Roy quickly decided to go. He tried to persuade me to come too. If we had been offered a job on a freighter out of San Francisco, I'm sure I would have gone with him to Australia. But going back up the coast I'd just come down from Portland, not knowing if I would be able to get a berth on a freighter . . . well, no thanks. Roy left for Vancouver Friday morning.

By now it appeared that I would not find a job in San Francisco. In that event, my plan had been to go on to my mother's cousin's farm near Riverside. I had enough money to bicycle another four hundred miles to get there. But after these past few days—first in San Rafael with my friend Doug, then in San Francisco, staying in the youth hostel and enjoying the company of the other young people—I did not want to go back on the road on my bike. And summer jobs might be as hard to find in the Los Angeles area as they were in San Francisco.

The good news was that my folks had received my airmailed request to wire me my last fifty dollars. I received the money on Thursday, July 14. I planned to spend two more days in San Francisco and then take the train home Sunday.

Late Friday morning I called the train station to buy a ticket. The ticket agent informed me that because the Democratic Convention had just ended in Los Angeles, all the train seats headed east out of San Francisco were booked for the next three days. The only remaining open seat available this week was on a Southern Pacific train leaving at 3:35 p.m. that very afternoon. I took it.

I called my friend Doug in San Rafael to tell him he could have my bike if he wanted to drive in to pick it up. I gathered up my other possessions, checked out of the hostel, and made it to the station in time to catch the 3:35 p.m. train out of San Francisco.

The train ride back to Michigan lasted two and a half days. We stopped for a while near Salt Lake City, where passengers were able to get off the train and walk around, and we changed trains in Chicago. Otherwise, I sat in a coach seat looking out the window at the empty plains and farmland by day; by night, hunched beside a darkened widow, I tried to sleep.

Monday morning was clear and sunny when I stepped off the train in Flint. I had twelve more miles to go and no bike. I did not call home. My mother did not drive, and my dad was working ten-hour days, seven days a week, on model year changeover in one of the auto plants. He needed the hours.

I started walking north on Saginaw Street while I considered what to do or who to call. I had made this walk before, as a child holding my mother's hand. In the late 1940s my mother and I would sometimes visit family in Canada when my dad was working, and we would take the train home from Stratford, Ontario, to Flint. When there was no one to meet us at the train station, Mother and I would walk the mile and a half or so north on Saginaw Street from the train station to the Greyhound bus station, located across from the Durant Hotel. Early in that hike, somewhere north of Twelfth Street, there was a toy store that had model trains running in the window. For me as a child, pausing at that window was the highlight of the trip home. Now, in 1960, the toy store was long gone, but the memory remained.

I reached Court Street and turned west toward Flushing. I kept walking. In the scale of things, walking the last twelve miles to Flushing fit comfortably with riding a bicycle to California. I was home by early afternoon, July 18, 1960. Mother was glad to see me safely home. But my dog, Boots, was gone.

Epilogue: The Journey

After returning home in the summer of 1960, I re-enrolled in Flint Junior College and finished the coursework for my associate's degree. I kept my grades up, but it was a struggle. Really, nothing had changed. The questions that had burdened me when I dropped out of college were still unanswered. What would I do? I had no career in mind. What contribution could I make, even with a college degree?

After graduating from junior college, I transferred to the University of Michigan–Flint, but any personal goal or sense of direction remained elusive. I dropped out of college again. As for the experience of the bicycle trip, it seemed not to have clarified anything, nor had it provided any greater self-awareness or direction in my life. I considered the bicycle trip a failure.

I found a second-shift job at a small company on the south end of Flint that made corrugated paper boxes. I made new friends. After the second shift ended at midnight, we would frequent the bars along South Saginaw Street. It wasn't North Beach, but we enjoyed the beer and the pool.

The summer of 1962 passed into fall. I did not re-enroll in college. The months drifted by for a year and a half. In the summer of 1963, I headed for Mexico with one of my second-shift friends. We had a fine adventure—Tampico, Mexico City, Acapulco—until I received a telegram from my dad bringing the news that I had been drafted into the army.

I did not expect to be drafted. It was August, 1963. Although the United States was providing aid to South Vietnamese soldiers, there were no American combat troops in Vietnam; the first ones would not be sent until 1965.

I was called up for two years of active duty. After basic training, I was assigned to an ordinance depot in upstate New York as a detachment clerk. A benefit of being drafted began to emerge: my responsibility for planning my own life had been suspended, taken out of my hands. I did not have to feel conflicted and guilty about not re-enrolling in college or finding a better job. My life had been hijacked. For the next two years, there was nothing I could do about it.

Once I settled in at the Seneca Army Depot, I rediscovered my personal curriculum, my reading list. I read Freud's *The Psychopathology of*

Everyday Life and *The Interpretation of Dreams*, Eric Fromm's *Escape from Freedom*, Nathanial West's *Miss Lonely Hearts*, and Jack Kerouac's *The Subterraneans*. I was startled to discover in the pages of Kerouac's novel a San Francisco that I had completely missed four years earlier. Ironically, my roommate Joe and his friend who invited me to go to North Beach with them may have recognized in me an affinity for that undiscovered San Francisco that I didn't recognize in myself.

In the fall of 1965, my two years of active duty were up. I returned home and went back to college. Something had changed in the three and a half years since I dropped out of college the second time. The existential questions "Who am I?" and "What contribution can I make?" had faded away. Life itself had begun to frame an identity for me. I focused on my coursework, made new friends, and met the girl who would eventually become my wife. Over the next three years I graduated, found a job, and got married. Life was good.

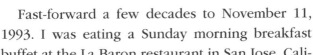

Fast-forward a few decades to November 11, 1993. I was eating a Sunday morning breakfast buffet at the La Baron restaurant in San Jose, California. I had been in San Jose all week attending a conference on technology in education, part of my job as a college administrator. This conference in San Jose was the first time I had been back to California since my bicycle trip to San Francisco thirty-three years earlier.

I had made no plans to revisit San Francisco. However, once in San Jose, old memories began to stir. I kept remembering the youth hostel I had stayed in on Jackson Street, Conard House. I wondered if I could find it.

When the conference wrapped up on Saturday I rented a car. My plan was to drive up the coast to San Francisco Sunday morning. I finished my breakfast at La Baron and headed for Santa Cruz. I reached Highway 1 and turned north to follow the coast road to San Francisco. It would be a day of exploration and reflection.

I stopped at Seal Rock just north of Santa Cruz

to watch the surfers. The drive up the coast was gorgeous, and wherever the beach was accessible, I could see surfers. I wished that my Irish friend Roy and I had tried California surfing thirty-three years earlier. In a sense, metaphorically, I had been a surfer; I'd climbed on my bike in Michigan and caught a ride to the coast. It was a great ride, but when the ride was over and the wave washed out on the shore, what was left?

Whenever I would tell others that I bicycled from Michigan to California at the age of nineteen, they would invariably see me as someone who accomplished a feat of cycling. Yes, I pedaled many hundred-mile days. I pedaled up mountains and into relentless headwinds. But I never thought of myself as a bicyclist. I was not trying to achieve a physical or athletic feat; I accepted rides in pickup trucks, a camper, and commercial haulers. Nor was my purpose to explore the many towns and cities I passed through, or to meet people, although I did meet many who were wonderful and generous. The trip was not about bicycling. I was on a journey to find myself.

I arrived in San Francisco by early afternoon. I found my way to Van Ness Avenue and followed it north to Jackson Street. I turned east and started looking for something familiar. When I reached the edge of Chinatown, I realized that I had turned the wrong way, so I headed back west on Jackson. By the 2000 block, the old Victorian row houses began to look familiar. I reached Alta Park and realized that I must have passed the house that had been the youth hostel. The grey Victorian row houses looked alike, and no sign identified one as Conard House. I parked on the street along the east side of Alta Park and set out to explore the area on foot.

Alta Park still offered that beautiful rooftops view of San Francisco, and the little market was still there on the corner of Fillmore and Jackson, where I bought food to take to the basement kitchen we travelers shared in Conard House. I could not, however, identify which of the similar looking Victorian houses on Jackson Street had been the youth hostel. I walked through the neighborhood, watching the people and looking in the store windows. As I walked south on Fillmore Street, a fifty-two-year-old attempting to retrace the steps of a nineteen-year-old, memories came rushing back—memories of all those days astride that bicycle, under the sun, riding into the tireless wind; memories of my Irish friend, my two New York roommates, and the other young travelers staying at Conard House; memories of bicycling through the San Francisco streets.

I began to feel uncomfortable, as if I was in someone else's space. I paused at a small restaurant. Through the window I could see empty tables with white tablecloths. I stepped in, chose a table by the window, and ordered a late lunch.

As I sat there watching the passers-by, a vivid image appeared to me beyond the window: a nineteen-year-old boy striding down the street. I was that boy—tall, lean, untouched by the years. The boy knew nothing of me. He was alone, walking along Fillmore Street into his unknowable future. I was frightened for him. I was in awe of his courage. I wondered what that boy went searching for on his long ride. Here I was in San Francisco, merely searching for a memory, and I beheld him in his present, striding into his future, a journey far more portentous than my afternoon search for a memory. "What right have I to claim him?" I thought. I had caught a glimpse of myself—something we are all searching for in our journeys, whether into the future or into the past.

Made in the USA
Columbia, SC
23 April 2018